Animal Show and Tell

Baby Animals

Élisabeth de Lambilly-Bresson

GARETH**STEVENS**

PUBLISHING

A Member of the WRC Media Family of Companies

The Kitten

I am a kitten.
I play with little things,
an acorn, a butterfly,
or a long piece of string.
I am cute and cuddly.
I can be your pet.
Meow!

The Fawn

I am a fawn.
You can see me
in the forest in spring.
But be very quiet!
Loud sounds frighten me.
Shhh!

The Duckling

I am a duckling.
I am a good follower.
You can see me following
my mother to the pond.
Quack!

The Donkey Foal

I am a donkey foal.
I am very lively,
but I can be stubborn, too.
Sometimes, even a tasty carrot
cannot make me change
my mind.
Hee-haw!

The Puppy

I am a puppy.
I am fuzzy and warm.
When I do not have a friend,
I am lonely.
Will you come play with me?
Woof!

The Lamb

I am a lamb.
My coat is wooly,
and my legs are wobbly.
I am afraid to be alone
so I stay close to my mother.
Ba-a-ah!

The Bear Cub

I am a bear cub.
I love to tumble and play.
I hunt for honey
and tasty ants.
Grrrr!

Please visit our Web site at: www.garethstevens.com
For a free color catalog describing Gareth Stevens Publishing's
list of high-quality books and multimedia programs, call
1-800-542-2595 (USA) or 1-800-387-3178 (Canada).
Gareth Stevens Publishing's fax: (414) 332-3567.

Library of Congress Cataloging-in-Publication Data

Lambilly-Bresson, Elisabeth de.
     [Tout doux! English]
     Baby animals / Elisabeth de Lambilly-Bresson. — North American ed.
          p. cm. — (Animal show and tell)
     ISBN-13: 978-0-8368-7835-6 (lib. bdg.)
     1. Animals—Infancy—Juvenile literature. I. Title.
     QL763.L3613   2007
     591.3'9—dc22   2006032933

This edition first published in 2007 by
Gareth Stevens Publishing
A Member of the WRC Media Family of Companies
330 West Olive Street, Suite 100
Milwaukee, WI 53212 USA

Translation: Valerie J. Weber
Gareth Stevens editor: Gini Holland
Gareth Stevens art direction and design: Tammy West

This edition copyright © 2007 by Gareth Stevens, Inc. Original edition copyright
© 2002 by Mango Jeunesse Press. First published as *Les animinis: Tout doux!*
by Mango Jeunesse Press.

Printed in the United States of America

1 2 3 4 5 6 7 8 9 10 10 09 08 07 06